MW01711496

the book of Psalms 51-100

ONE CHAPTER A DAY

GoodMorningGirls.org

Psalms 51-100

Welcome! We are so glad you are joining us.

God created us to walk with Him, to know Him, and to be loved by Him. He is our living well, and when we drink from the water He continually provides, His living water will change the entire course of our lives.

> *Jesus said: "Whoever drinks of the water that I will give him will never be thirsty again. The water that I will give him will become in him a spring of water welling up to eternal life." ~ John 4:14 (ESV)*

So let's begin.

The method we use here at GMG is called the **SOAK** method.

- ❒ **S**—The S stands for ***Scripture***—Read the chapter for the day. Then choose 1-2 verses and write them out word for word. (There is no right or wrong choice—just let the Holy Spirit guide you.)
- ❒ **O**—The O stands for ***Observation***—Look at the verse or verses you wrote out. Write 1 or 2 observations. What stands out to you? What do you learn about the character of God from these verses? Is there a promise, command or teaching?
- ❒ **A**—The A stands for ***Application***—Personalize the verses. What is God saying to you? How can you apply them to your life? Are there any changes you need to make or an action to take?
- ❒ **K**—The K stands for ***Kneeling in Prayer***—Pause, kneel and pray. Confess any sin God has revealed to you today. Praise God for His word. Pray the passage over your own life or someone you love. Ask God to help you live out your applications.

SOAK God's word into your heart and squeeze every bit of nourishment you can out of each day's scripture reading. Soon you will find your life transformed by the renewing of your mind!

Walk with the King!

Courtney

WomenLivingWell.org, GoodMorningGuys.org

GMG Bible Coloring Chart

COLORS	KEYWORDS
PURPLE	God, Jesus, Holy Spirit, Saviour, Messiah
PINK	women of the Bible, family, marriage, parenting, friendship, relationships
RED	love, kindness, mercy, compassion, peace, grace
GREEN	faith, obedience, growth, fruit, salvation, fellowship, repentance
YELLOW	worship, prayer, praise, doctrine, angels, miracles,power of God, blessings
BLUE	wisdom, teaching, instruction, commands
ORANGE	prophecy, history, times, places, kings, genealogies, people, numbers, covenants, vows, visions, oaths, future
BROWN/GRAY	Satan, sin, death, hell, evil, idols, false teachers, hypocrisy, temptation

Introduction to the Book of Psalms

Down through the centuries, believers have turned to the book of Psalms, as their favorite book of the Bible. Do you need encouragement, comfort, guidance, healing, courage or joy?

Read the book of Psalms.

The depth of emotion expressed by the writers makes this book relatable, encouraging, and comforting. It is a collection of poems, hymns, songs and prayers. They express deep and sincere faith in the midst of trials and tribulations.

The Hebrew word for "psalms" means "to pluck". This implies that the Psalms were to be accompanied by a stringed instrument. The poetic rhythm and figurative language used, clearly expresses the emotion the writer was feeling.

In the New Testament, believers are instructed to sing psalms:

> Ephesians 5:19 says, *"address one another in **psalms** and hymns and spiritual songs, singing and making melody to the Lord with your heart."*
>
> Colossians 3:16 says, *"Let the word of Christ dwell in you richly, teaching and admonishing one another in all wisdom, singing **psalms** and hymns and spiritual songs, with thankfulness in your hearts to God."*

Though this book was written many years ago, it is still relevant to believers today.

The Purpose: The book of Psalms was to be used as a hymnbook to sing praises to God. The word psalms is associated with playing instruments to accompany these songs.

The Author: The name of the author is at the start of each psalm. David is the most frequent writer. Other authors include: Solomon, Moses, the Sons of Korah, Asaph, Ethan and Ezahite. Some psalms have no designated author.

Time Period: This book was written between 1410-450 B.C.

Key Verse: Psalm 8:9

O Lord, our Lord, how majestic is your name in all the earth!

The Outline:

Originally, the book of Psalms was divided into 5 different books according to what was found within them.

- Book 1—Psalms 1-41
- Book 2—Psalms 42-72
- Book 3—Psalms 73-89
- Book 4—Psalms 90-106
- Book 5—Psalms 107-150

Types of Psalms:

- Psalms of Thanksgiving and Praise
- Psalms of Lament
- Psalms of Meditation, Prayer and Petition
- Psalms of Confidence and Trust
- Wisdom Psalms that Teach
- Historical Psalms
- Psalms of Suffering and Tears
- Imprecatory Psalms—Psalms that invoke judgment on their enemies.
- Kingship Psalms—Psalms that point to the future Messiah—the King of Kings or speak of David as a king.
- Acrostic Psalms—These psalms are written with special patterns using the Hebrew alphabet.

The book of Psalms is a hymnal, a prayer book, and a training guide. Every emotion a man can have is expressed from joy and sadness to anger, fear, doubt, repentance, praise, and trust. If you've felt it, Psalms expresses it. We could spend the rest of our lives reading the book of Psalms over and over and still not mine the depth of all that this book offers.

So let's get started!

Keep walking with the King!

Courtney

Create in me a clean heart, O God,
and renew a right spirit within me.
Psalm 51:10

Reflection Question:

Psalm 51 is one of the most powerful laments in all of scripture. King David had fallen into the sin of adultery with Bathsheba and now his eyes were opened to his sin. As he repents before God, he leans on God's great love and mercy for forgiveness and he asks the Lord to create in him a clean heart.

David didn't want an old heart that was being remodeled or renovated, he wanted a new heart that was pure. He wanted a renewed spirit that was steadfast in doing what was right. Pause and reflect on your own life right now. Is there a sin that you need to repent of or an area where you need God to renew your spirit? Write it below, pray over it and remember your God is abundantly merciful and loves you so. You are forgiven and clean and are freed by the blood of the lamb!

Psalm 51

S—The S stands for ***Scripture***

O—The O stands for ***Observation***

A—The A stands for ***Application***

K—The K stands for ***Kneeling in Prayer***

I trust in the steadfast love of God forever and ever.
Psalm 52:8

Reflection Question:

While this Psalm is specifically about David and Doeg, who was a boastful wicked man, it is relevant to us. While others may lie and deceive and trust in their riches or themselves, the righteous wait on the Lord and trust in the steadfast love of God.

Have you had a conflict with someone lately? In times of conflict, it is easy to feel frustration, confusion, and heartache but for the godly, we can release it in prayer and trust God to take care of the outcome. How does God's steadfast love for you help you in a season of conflict and in what ways do you need to trust God more?

Psalm 52

S—The S stands for ***Scripture***

O—The O stands for ***Observation***

A—The A stands for ***Application***

K—The K stands for ***Kneeling in Prayer***

God looks down from heaven to
see if there are any who understand,
who seek after God.
Psalm 53:2

Reflection Question:

David reflects on those who reject God and calls them fools. It's interesting to note where they deny God—it's in their hearts. Verse 2 says the Lord is looking down from heaven to see if there are any who seek him.

We may have a lot of intellectual knowledge about God but ultimately our decisions are made by the passions of our heart. How is your heart today? Is it seeking God or seeking pleasure and how can you realign your heart with the heart of God?

Psalm 53

S—The S stands for ***Scripture***

O—The O stands for ***Observation***

A—The A stands for ***Application***

K—The K stands for ***Kneeling in Prayer***

Behold, God is my helper;
the Lord is the upholder of my life.
Psalm 54:4

Reflection Question:

While David was on the run from his enemies, he confidently trusted in God's help. His fears and struggles did not cause him to question the goodness of God but rather gave him strength, as he trusted that God was the one holding him up.

Write down a time when you know that God helped you through something you were struggling with. Is there something difficult you are facing today? How does remembering that God is your helper and the upholder of your life, encourage you as you face your current struggles?

Psalm 54

S—The S stands for ***Scripture***

O—The O stands for ***Observation***

A—The A stands for ***Application***

K—The K stands for ***Kneeling in Prayer***

Cast your burden on the Lord,
and he will sustain you;
he will never permit
the righteous to be moved.
Psalm 55:22

Reflection Question:

Few things are harder to bear than the betrayal of a close friend. David knew this was a burden he could not carry on his own. He had to give it over to the Lord in faith. In exchange for his burden, he received the strength to be sustained and not moved.

Is there someone you love who has betrayed you? This is too much to bear on your own. The Lord wants you to give this burden to Him and for you to trust him to sustain you and heal you. Write a prayer below handing over this relationship to God.

Psalm 55

S—The S stands for ***Scripture***

O—The O stands for ***Observation***

A—The A stands for ***Application***

K—The K stands for ***Kneeling in Prayer***

You have kept count of my tossing;
put my tears in your bottle...
This I know, that God is for me.
Psalm 56:8, 9

Reflection Question:

David was all alone, but he took great comfort in knowing that God saw his sorrow and tears. His tossing and turning and tears on his bed did not mean that God was against him. He knew that God was for him and heard his cries for help.

What was the last thing you cried over? How does knowing that God sees every tear make you feel? Do you need reminded today that God is for you? God is for you and He loves you. Never forget that! Keep trusting in Him!

Psalm 56

S—The S stands for ***Scripture***

O—The O stands for ***Observation***

A—The A stands for ***Application***

K—The K stands for ***Kneeling in Prayer***

Be exalted, O God, above the heavens!
Let your glory be over all the earth!
Psalm 57:11

Reflection Question:

David wrote this Psalm while he was in a cave hiding from Saul. Even though David had cried out to God and his circumstances had not changed, he praised God. David's spirit was free even though he was stuck in a cave.

In the midst of hard times, it is tempting to fall into despair as we wait on the Lord. Are you in the midst of a hard trial today? Free yourself through praise. Write 5 things below that you can praise God for today.

Psalm 57

S—The S stands for ***Scripture***

O—The O stands for ***Observation***

A—The A stands for ***Application***

K—The K stands for ***Kneeling in Prayer***

Mankind will say,
"Surely there is a reward
for the righteous;
surely there is a God
who judges on earth."
Psalm 58:11

Reflection Question:

David was lamenting over all the injustice in this world and longing for God to act on his behalf. One day, at the last judgement, there will be justice and the righteous will be rewarded and the wicked denied.

When those who do evil succeed and those who do what is right seem to suffer, it can shake our faith. But we are promised that one day we will receive a reward. How does it encourage you and give you hope to know that a reward in heaven awaits you?

Psalm 58

S—The S stands for ***Scripture***

O—The O stands for ***Observation***

A—The A stands for ***Application***

K—The K stands for ***Kneeling in Prayer***

But I will sing of your strength;
I will sing aloud of your
steadfast love in the morning.
For you have been to me a fortress
and a refuge in the day of my distress.
Psalm 59:16

Reflection Question:

This Psalm begins with David praying and asking the Lord for protection and it ends with David singing about God's steadfast love in the morning. Sometimes when the night is long, we wonder if we will make it until morning. But when day breaks and the sun rises, we must lift our eyes to Jesus and thank him for bringing us through the darkness.

While those who are evil spend their days stirring up strife with "swords in their lips" (v. 7), God's people are to be found singing praises. David's confidence that God would protect him from evil gave him the strength to sing, even in the midst of his fears. Do you sing praises when you are fearful? Is this something you need to do more? How does singing praises to God change your outlook and give you strength?

Psalm 59

S—The S stands for ***Scripture***

O—The O stands for ***Observation***

A—The A stands for ***Application***

K—The K stands for ***Kneeling in Prayer***

With God we shall do valiantly;
it is he who will tread down our foes.
Psalm 60:12

Reflection Question:

David wanted more than just the help of man, he knew he needed God for victory. David also knew that he could not sit and wait for God to fight his battles for him. He needed to courageously fight alongside God.

God fights for us on two fronts. Not only does he help us, but he suppresses the enemy as well. What battle in your own life have you been fighting in your own strength? Go to God and ask him to help you and then bravely face your battle through the strength of God.

Psalm 60

S—The S stands for ***Scripture***

O—The O stands for ***Observation***

A—The A stands for ***Application***

K—The K stands for ***Kneeling in Prayer***

Hear my cry, O God,
listen to my prayer;
from the end of the earth I call to you
when my heart is faint.
Psalm 61:1, 2

Reflection Question:

David cried out to God "from the end of the earth," yet he was never far from the Promised Land. Figuratively speaking, his heart was at the end of the earth. He was weary and on the brink of despair as he cried out to God to lead him and protect him.

Have you been worn out and tired by the difficulties of daily life and suffered from feeling distant from God? David did not give up hope or deny God's love in the midst of these feelings, instead he cried out to God and drew near to him. We have a great King who is always with us. Pray and ask God to guide you with wisdom and strength today in the midst of your weariness.

Psalm 61

S—The S stands for ***Scripture***

O—The O stands for ***Observation***

A—The A stands for ***Application***

K—The K stands for ***Kneeling in Prayer***

If riches increase,
set not your heart on them.
Psalm 62:10

Reflection Question:

David went from being an average shepherd boy to a wealthy king. David's riches had increased over his lifetime, but he had learned that it was foolish to trust in them. He was able to have great wealth without setting his heart and affections on them.

Is money a struggle for you? Perhaps you are in need of more or maybe you are in a season of plenty. Either way, money can become a fixation of our hearts if we do not guard our hearts. Money is not to be our source of joy, our source of security or a source of pride. In what ways do you struggle to trust in God more than money and how can you trust God more today?

Psalm 62

S—The S stands for ***Scripture***

O—The O stands for ***Observation***

A—The A stands for ***Application***

K—The K stands for ***Kneeling in Prayer***

O God, you are my God;
earnestly I seek you;
my soul thirsts for you.
Psalm 63:1

Reflection Question:

The thirst of David's soul led him to earnestly seek after God. Like a man who is thirsty in a dry desert land, he sought God and found satisfaction for his soul, in God. In verse 5, David compares beholding God's glory with the satisfaction of eating the richest of foods. Our God is so good!

What do you earnestly seek after? Look at your calendar and finances and you can quickly see where your priorities lie. We must never seek satisfaction in the things of this world, or we will find ourselves in an emotional desert. Even our bodies feel the effects of our emotional deserts. Is your soul thirsty? How can you make God more of a priority in your life?

Psalm 63

S—The S stands for ***Scripture***

O—The O stands for ***Observation***

A—The A stands for ***Application***

K—The K stands for ***Kneeling in Prayer***

Hide me from the secret
plots of the wicked...
who whet their tongues like swords,
who aim bitter words like arrows.
Psalm 64:2, 3

Reflection Question:

David knew that behind his back, in secret places, people were talking about him. They were making plans against him and telling lies about him. He was powerless to stop them, so he prayed. Though he did not know what was being said about him, God did.

Sometimes it's easier when things are said right out in the open to our face rather than behind our back. A hidden sniper in battle is much more dangerous than a man out in the open. Have you suffered from rumors and lies being said about you in secret places? Though in the moment, it may seem that their words are winning, God has a good plan for you and he will not let you down. He is with you. Say a prayer now asking God to protect you from any secret gossip that could harm you.

Psalm 64

S—The S stands for ***Scripture***

O—The O stands for ***Observation***

A—The A stands for ***Application***

K—The K stands for ***Kneeling in Prayer***

You make the going out of the morning and the evening to shout for joy.
Psalm 65:8

Reflection Question:

We see the awesomeness of our God in creation! Verse 6 says that God stills the roaring of the waves and seas. Our God is strong! He lovingly takes care of the earth, making sure it has all that it needs with both water and grain. He makes the sun rise in the morning and gives us moonlight at night.

When we pause and consider the greatness of God in creation, we cannot help but to rejoice. He fills the hills with cattle, the meadows with flocks, and the valleys with grain. After showers of rain and a season of growth, wagons overflow with an abundance of food. Consider all of this and don't just sing praise to God—shout praise! How does considering the goodness of God in creation, lead you to joy?

Psalm 65

S—The S stands for ***Scripture***

O—The O stands for ***Observation***

A—The A stands for ***Application***

K—The K stands for ***Kneeling in Prayer***

Come and hear,
all you who fear God,
and I will tell what he has done for my soul.
Psalm 66:16

Reflection Question:

The Lord had brought David through a season of suffering and now he was offering a burnt sacrifice to the Lord. David had remained faithful through his trial and he didn't just want to give God a sacrifice of thanks, but he also wanted to share with all those who would hear, what God had done.

Has God brought you through a recent season of suffering or testing? God uses our tests to become a testimony and our messes to become a message for others. What has God brought you through? List some of the things God has done for your soul and then pray about who you can share this with.

Psalm 66

S—The S stands for ***Scripture***

O—The O stands for ***Observation***

A—The A stands for ***Application***

K—The K stands for ***Kneeling in Prayer***

May God be gracious to us and bless us and make his face to shine upon us.
Psalm 67:1

Reflection Question:

The Psalmist knew his sinfulness and his need for grace and mercy but more than that, he longed for God's blessing. There is nothing greater than God's face shining upon us. God's presence is with us and because of Jesus' sacrifice on the cross, we are God's children and He is watching over us with a smile.

When someone dislikes us, they either look away from us or give looks that show disgust, but a smiling face turned toward you, shines. It is personal, warm and friendly. So How does it make you feel to know that the all-powerful creator of our world, is watching over you with his glorious face turned toward you?

Psalm 67

S—The S stands for ***Scripture***

O—The O stands for ***Observation***

A—The A stands for ***Application***

K—The K stands for ***Kneeling in Prayer***

Father of the fatherless
and protector of widows
is God in his holy habitation.
Psalm 68:5, 6

Reflection Question:

David sees God's mighty hand, not just in his military battles, but also in his care for the weak and lonely. God becomes what his people need. If they need strength for a battle, he gives them strength. If they need a father, he is their heavenly father. If they need protection, he gives protection.

We are not alone. God acts on the behalf of his people no matter what the need is.

The rulers of this world surround themselves with the rich and famous, but God serves those who are in need. How have you seen God be a father to the fatherless or the protection for a widow that you know? Do you have a need today? Tell it to God in prayer.

Psalm 68

S—The S stands for ***Scripture***

O—The O stands for ***Observation***

A—The A stands for ***Application***

K—The K stands for ***Kneeling in Prayer***

Save me, O God!
For the waters
have come up to my neck.
Psalm 69:1

Reflection Question:

David felt like he was drowning in his sea of troubles. He had no secure place to set his feet, while the floods of life overwhelmed him. He wearied himself crying out for the Lord and waiting on God.

When troubles flood our lives, it is easy to become overwhelmed and discouraged. When we are weary, we are tempted to look for solutions through friends or scrolling on-line but David cried out to the Lord to save him, to answer him, to turn to him (v.16), to not hide his face from him (v.17) and to draw near to him (v. 18). Who or what do you usually turn to first, when you are overwhelmed? How can you more earnestly seek God when you feel like you are sinking in life?

Psalm 69

S—The S stands for ***Scripture***

O—The O stands for ***Observation***

A—The A stands for ***Application***

K—The K stands for ***Kneeling in Prayer***

"God is great!"
Psalm 70:4

Reflection Question:

David says, that all who seek God should rejoice and be glad in Him and say, "God is great!"

God cannot be compared with anything in all of creation because he is the creator. He is superior to all things. He is wiser, mightier and more majestic than all. When was the last time you said out loud, "God is great!" Tell him right now how great He is and then make it a point today to tell someone else, that God is great.

Psalm 70

S—The S stands for ***Scripture***

O—The O stands for ***Observation***

A—The A stands for ***Application***

K—The K stands for ***Kneeling in Prayer***

So even to old age and gray hairs,
O God, do not forsake me,
until I proclaim your might to another generation.
Psalm 71:18

Reflection Question:

David had the privilege of knowing God since youth and he prayed that God's favor would continue to be with him, into old age. He wanted to tell the next generation about God's might.

As we grow older, we can be tempted to grow colder and more cynical because of the trials we have suffered in life. But there is great value in godly men and women telling stories of how God helped them through their difficulties. This gives courage to the next generation. Who do you know that is younger than you, that you can encourage? Pray and ask the Lord to give you an opportunity to tell your stories and strengthen the next generation.

Psalm 71

S—The S stands for ***Scripture***

O—The O stands for ***Observation***

A—The A stands for ***Application***

K—The K stands for ***Kneeling in Prayer***

Blessed be the Lord,
the God of Israel,
who alone does wondrous things.
Psalm 72:18

Reflection Question:

Originally, Psalms was divided into 5 different books and so Psalm 72 is the end of book number two. This Psalm ends with a doxology. In the Greek, doxa means "glory and splendor" and logos means "word or speaking". And so this spoken word of praise, brings us to the end of book two. It is interesting to note that Solomon wrote Psalm 72 and in verse 20, he refers to his father David—not as a King, but rather humbly as the son of Jesse, who was once just a shepherd boy.

It is beautiful to see that just like his father David, Solomon experienced the wonders of God. David had successfully handed his baton of faith to the next generation. What is your legacy? How are you passing your faith to the next generation?

Psalm 72

S—The S stands for ***Scripture***

O—The O stands for ***Observation***

A—The A stands for ***Application***

K—The K stands for ***Kneeling in Prayer***

My flesh and my heart may fail,
but God is the strength of my heart
and my portion forever.
Psalm 73:26

Reflection Question:

This Psalm begins and ends by the writer declaring that God is good yet in the middle, he wrestles with the success of those who do wrong. In verse 23, he encourages himself by remembering that God is continually with him and holding his hand.

Sometimes in our flesh, we are worn out and discouraged, especially when we see those who are doing evil prosper. How does remembering that God is with you and you are with him, encourage your weary heart? How is God your strength in troubled times?

Psalm 73

S—The S stands for ***Scripture***

O—The O stands for ***Observation***

A—The A stands for ***Application***

K—The K stands for ***Kneeling in Prayer***

Yours is the day, yours also the night;
you have established the heavenly
lights and the sun.
You have fixed all the
boundaries of the earth;
you have made summer and winter.
Psalm 74:16, 17

Reflection Question:

God made both day and night and all of the seasons. They are meant to be blessings. He knows exactly what we need. Sometimes we need to work hard and at other times, we need rest.

All of our time and seasons are in God's hands. How does knowing that God is lovingly in control of the sun, moon, stars, clouds and sunshine comfort you?

Psalm 74

S—The S stands for ***Scripture***

O—The O stands for ***Observation***

A—The A stands for ***Application***

K—The K stands for ***Kneeling in Prayer***

We give thanks to you, O God;
we give thanks, for your name is near.
We recount your wondrous deeds.
Psalm 75:1

Reflection Question:

The repetition of thanks in Psalm 75 reminds us that we are to give God thanks over and over and over again. It is a wonderful thing to experience the nearness of God!

To recount the wondrous deeds of God, is to tell the story of our experiences and give thanks. Write below about a time when you experienced the wonder of the nearness of God.

Psalm 75

S—The S stands for ***Scripture***

O—The O stands for ***Observation***

A—The A stands for ***Application***

K—The K stands for ***Kneeling in Prayer***

But you, you are to be feared!
Who can stand before you?
Psalm 76:7

Reflection Question:

Our reverence and honor of God is to go beyond just our praise. He is to be feared, as we stand in awe of his power and might.

Pause and imagine yourself before the throne of God. What would you do? What would you say?

Psalm 76

S—The S stands for ***Scripture***

O—The O stands for ***Observation***

A—The A stands for ***Application***

K—The K stands for ***Kneeling in Prayer***

In the day of my trouble
I seek the Lord.
Psalm 77:2

Reflection Question:

When the Psalmist was in trouble, he did not seek comfort from a friend, food or fun but rather—he sought the Lord. And when God still seemed distant, he remembered the days of old, the songs of praise he used to sing, and the things God had done for him in the past. This encouraged his soul.

It is when God seems the farthest from us, that we must seek him until we find him.

God wants us to seek him out and encourage ourselves by remembering the things he has done for us in the past. Where do you turn in times of trouble? Do you tend to forget what God has already done for you and how do memories from the past encourage you?

Psalm 77

S—The S stands for ***Scripture***

O—The O stands for ***Observation***

A—The A stands for ***Application***

K—The K stands for ***Kneeling in Prayer***

Tell the coming generation
the glorious deeds of the Lord,
and his might,
and the wonders that he has done.
Psalm 78:4

Reflection Question:

The Psalmist wanted to pass on three things to the next generation: the story of God's glorious deeds, the truth of God's might and the wonderful works God had done. Psalm 78 is honest about the weaknesses and failures of God's people. He wanted to pass on the stories about God's strength, not the stories of strong people.

When was the last time you told someone in the generation behind you, a story about something God has done? How can you work on revealing the strength of God in your stories rather than the strength of people?

Psalm 78

S—The S stands for ***Scripture***

O—The O stands for ***Observation***

A—The A stands for ***Application***

K—The K stands for ***Kneeling in Prayer***

Help us, O God of our salvation,
for the glory of your name;
deliver us, and atone for our sins,
for your name's sake!
Psalm 79:9

Reflection Question:

When the Psalmist cried out for deliverance, he acknowledged his sins and appealed to the glory of God for help. He knew people everywhere were watching and so it was for God's name sake that he wanted to see his people helped by their mighty God.

Often times, when we cry out to God for help, it is motivated simply by our own desire to be saved from something difficult. We simply cry out "God help me!" But have we considered the higher purpose of God's glory and his name sake? How does it change your prayers to make it about God rather than yourself?

Psalm 79

S—The S stands for ***Scripture***

O—The O stands for ***Observation***

A—The A stands for ***Application***

K—The K stands for ***Kneeling in Prayer***

Restore us,
O Lord God of hosts!
Let your face shine,
that we may be saved!
Psalm 80:19

Reflection Question:

Three times in this Psalm, the Psalmist asked for God's restoration and presence. Revival begins when God's people turn towards God and God's face shines brightly on them. This prayer has been ultimately answered in Christ who restores us, saves us and causes God's grace and favor to shine on us.

Our God is the Lord God of hosts. This is no one greater and he is with us. He wants to restore us and save us. How have you experienced the goodness and presence of God in your life?

Psalm 80

S—The S stands for ***Scripture***

O—The O stands for ***Observation***

A—The A stands for ***Application***

K—The K stands for ***Kneeling in Prayer***

In distress you called,
and I delivered you;
I answered you in the
secret place of thunder.
Psalm 81:7

Reflection Question:

Thunder is frequently used as a metaphor for God's presence or voice. All of us understand the power of thunder trembling as lightening releases. This is a picture of our God's power, might and authority.

Think about the last time you heard thunder outside. I don't mean the distant rumble of thunder, but the wall shaking, window rattling strikes of thunder you have heard in the past. Now consider...the God of the thunder is in complete control and you are loved by a God, whose voice thunders. How does this change your outlook on your prayers to him?

Psalm 81

S—The S stands for ***Scripture***

O—The O stands for ***Observation***

A—The A stands for ***Application***

K—The K stands for ***Kneeling in Prayer***

God has taken his place
in the divine council;
in the midst of the gods
he holds judgment.
Psalm 82:1

Reflection Question:

The Psalmist gives us a picture of God standing in the midst of those who are strong and in authority on earth. God will judge the leaders, kings and false gods. While they think they are mighty and strong, it is ultimately God who determines their fate.

The injustices of this world are disheartening. People long for a good leader who will right wrongs and protect their nation. How does knowing that all authorities here on earth are accountable to God in the end, bring you peace?

Psalm 82

S—The S stands for ***Scripture***

O—The O stands for ***Observation***

A—The A stands for ***Application***

K—The K stands for ***Kneeling in Prayer***

That they may know that you alone,
whose name is the Lord,
are the Most High over all the earth.
Psalm 83:18

Reflection Question:

This Psalm is a redemptive prayer for God to not stay silent but rather make himself known, so that even his enemies would seek Him and know that he is the Most High over all the earth.

Jesus told us to pray for our enemies (Matt. 5:43-45). And this Psalm shows us that when we pray for them, we can pray redemption for them. Is there someone in your life that you consider an enemy? Write a prayer below for them and in it include a plea that they would seek God and know him.

Psalm 83

S—The S stands for ***Scripture***

O—The O stands for ***Observation***

A—The A stands for ***Application***

K—The K stands for ***Kneeling in Prayer***

For the Lord God is a sun and shield;
the Lord bestows favor and honor.
No good thing does he withhold
from those who walk uprightly.
Psalm 84:11

Reflection Question:

For those who delight in being close to the Lord, God is a sun and a shield. The sun represents blessings and the shield represents safety and security. The Lord does not withhold good things from those who walk uprightly.

Are you walking closely with the Lord right now? What blessings or good things have you experienced as a result of walking closely with God?

Psalm 84

S—The S stands for ***Scripture***

O—The O stands for ***Observation***

A—The A stands for ***Application***

K—The K stands for ***Kneeling in Prayer***

Steadfast love and faithfulness meet;
righteousness and peace kiss each other.
Psalm 85:10

Reflection Question:

A picture of closeness and intimacy is shown as love and faithfulness meet and then righteousness and peace kiss each other.

God's love, faithfulness, righteousness and peace all come together on the cross. In the Garden of Eden, when man fell, these four things were lost but through God's great work of salvation, we are restored. As believers we have received all of these attributes. Which of these four attributes have you experienced most lately and in what ways?

Psalm 85

S—The S stands for ***Scripture***

O—The O stands for ***Observation***

A—The A stands for ***Application***

K—The K stands for ***Kneeling in Prayer***

For you, O Lord,
are good and forgiving,
abounding in steadfast love
to all who call upon you.
Psalm 86:5

Reflection Question:

David trusted in the goodness and forgiveness of God. He knew that God was full of abounding steadfast love and he trusted that when he called on the Lord, the Lord was there for Him.

In the midst of trials, are you sometimes tempted to doubt the goodness of God? How does remembering God's forgiveness and abounding love for you, reveal God's goodness to you.

Psalm 86

S—The S stands for ***Scripture***

O—The O stands for ***Observation***

A—The A stands for ***Application***

K—The K stands for ***Kneeling in Prayer***

Glorious things of you are spoken,
O city of God.
Psalm 87:3

Reflection Question:

God chose the city of Zion, Jerusalem, to reveal his glory. God is omnipresent. He is everywhere, yet Jerusalem was chosen as a special city of God, where the atonement for all of the world's sins took place. There was glorious worship offered there and a God's special presence was there.

God met his people in an intimate way in Zion. But God also meet us right where we are today. That's our glorious God! Where is your favorite place to meet with God and why do you love that place so much?

Psalm 87

S—The S stands for ***Scripture***

O—The O stands for ***Observation***

A—The A stands for ***Application***

K—The K stands for ***Kneeling in Prayer***

O Lord, God of my salvation,
I cry out day and night before you.
Psalm 88:1

Reflection Question:

It is said of this Psalm, that it is the saddest and most depressed of all laments. Unlike most Psalms that end in praise, this one does not. The writer feels as if the hand of God is against him and his only comfort is that the Lord is his salvation.

In Job 13:15 Job said: ***"Though he slay me, yet will I trust in him."*** I love this deep faith that Job had even in the midst of his darkness. Have you ever felt like the hand of the Lord was against you? What made you feel that way? How does remembering your salvation shine light into the darkness when you have these feelings?

Psalm 88

S—The S stands for ***Scripture***

O—The O stands for ***Observation***

A—The A stands for ***Application***

K—The K stands for ***Kneeling in Prayer***

I will sing of the steadfast love
of the Lord, forever;
with my mouth I will make known your
faithfulness to all generations.
Psalm 89:1

Reflection Question:

God's steadfast love lasts forever and ever and so we should praise him forever and ever. We should tell of his faithfulness to the next generation. Not only do we want to experience his love and faithfulness, but we want others to experience it too!

This Psalm may open with praise, but it is a lament. When we are going through hard times, we tend to complain but complaining never eases our troubles. How does choosing joy change our perspective in life. List below three things you can praise God for today.

Psalm 89

S—The S stands for ***Scripture***

O—The O stands for ***Observation***

A—The A stands for ***Application***

K—The K stands for ***Kneeling in Prayer***

Teach us to number our days
that we may get a heart of wisdom.
Psalm 90:12

Reflection Question:

Of all the math we do in our lifetime, this is the most important, numbering our days. In Bible times, men would number their sheep, oxen, harvest and coins, but rarely did a man number his days. It is something we must be taught to do and it's not a mind exercise—it's a heart one. We don't do it naturally, but it leads to wisdom as we remember how short life is.

Pause for a moment and do the math. If you live to be 80, how many years do you have left? Now multiply that number by 365. How many days do you have left? What if the years are only 70 total—now how many days do you have left? Life is short and uncertain. How can you live more wisely and for eternity, in the days you have left?

Psalm 90

S—The S stands for ***Scripture***

O—The O stands for ***Observation***

A—The A stands for ***Application***

K—The K stands for ***Kneeling in Prayer***

He who dwells in the shelter
of the Most High
will abide in the shadow of the
Almighty.
Psalm 91:1

Reflection Question:

A dwelling is a place where we live or reside. For those who live and dwell close to God, we experience God as a shelter. We are under his protection, comfort and care.

Some only run to God for shelter when they face hard times. But to dwell and abide with God means to walk closely with him every single day. It is only then that God's shadow can fall on us. Are you dwelling with God or just visiting him from time to time? How can you walk more closely with him this week and live under the shadow of the Almighty?

Psalm 91

S—The S stands for ***Scripture***

O—The O stands for ***Observation***

A—The A stands for ***Application***

K—The K stands for ***Kneeling in Prayer***

It is good to sing praises
to your name, O Most High;
to declare your steadfast
love in the morning,
and your faithfulness by night.
Psalm 92:1, 2

Reflection Question:

Singing praises to God is good. It is not just good to God, but it is good for the worshipper's soul as well. It frees our spirits as we lift our voices up day and night. At night, we have more to praise God for than in the morning because we have one more day of life experiencing God's faithfulness.

Do you find yourself singing praises early in the morning? How about late at night, at the end of the day? What keeps you from singing out to God more throughout the day?

Psalm 92

S—The S stands for ***Scripture***

O—The O stands for ***Observation***

A—The A stands for ***Application***

K—The K stands for ***Kneeling in Prayer***

Mightier than the thunders
of many waters,
mightier than the waves of the sea,
the Lord on high is mighty!
Psalm 93:4

Reflection Question:

The sound of waves thundering and crashing against the shores is loud and mighty. The depths of the ocean are fathomless and when there are storms, no man can stop the raging seas. The ocean holds many dangers and pitfalls just as our life does but there is none that is stronger than God.

God's wisdom and might is above all that we face in life. How does this picture of God being mightier than the waves of the ocean, comfort you in the midst of your challenges or difficulties today? How does knowing that even the winds and the waves obey God, give you peace?

Psalm 93

S—The S stands for ***Scripture***

O—The O stands for ***Observation***

A—The A stands for ***Application***

K—The K stands for ***Kneeling in Prayer***

When I thought, “My foot slips,” your steadfast love, O Lord, held me up.
Psalm 94:18

Reflection Question:

When the Psalmist’s foot had slipped, it was God who was there holding him up. Perhaps he slipped into fear or the temptation to not trust in God. God’s steadfast love for his people is unconditional and he is there for us, even when we slip up.

When we are feeling weak, sometimes we slip but God is with us and he prevents us from falling into ruin. Think of a time when you slipped but God held you up and write about it below. Give thanks to God for his steadfast love that is daily helping us.

Psalm 94

S—The S stands for ***Scripture***

O—The O stands for ***Observation***

A—The A stands for ***Application***

K—The K stands for ***Kneeling in Prayer***

Oh come, let us worship and bow down; let us kneel before the Lord, our Maker.
Psalm 95:6

Reflection Question:

While it is good to worship alone, it is also good to worship God in community. This Psalm emphasizes twice the humble act of bowing and kneeling down to the Lord. He is the King of Kings and above all creation. He is our maker and worthy of our humble adoration.

In scripture, we see many different forms of worship from singing, to clapping, to dancing, to shouting, to playing harps and tambourines (and other instruments), to lifting holy hands, bowing down and even falling to the ground in awe. All of these ways are pleasing to the Lord, as long as we come with a sincere heart of humility. Which of these acts of worship do you practice most? Today when you pray, I encourage you to kneel. How does kneeling intensify your prayers?

Psalm 95

S—The S stands for ***Scripture***

O—The O stands for ***Observation***

A—The A stands for ***Application***

K—The K stands for ***Kneeling in Prayer***

Oh sing to the Lord
a new song.
Psalm 96:1

Reflection Question:

Praise is not meant to be a dull routine of repetition. Instead, as we receive new mercies from God each day and learn new things about his love and grace, our songs should be fresh and new.

Have you fallen into a boring routine of singing the same songs over and over? What new things have you experienced or learned about God that you can celebrate and turn into a new song?

Psalm 96

S—The S stands for ***Scripture***

O—The O stands for ***Observation***

A—The A stands for ***Application***

K—The K stands for ***Kneeling in Prayer***

O you who love the Lord,
hate evil!
Psalm 97:10

Reflection Question:

When we consider how great and mighty and highly exalted our God is, it changes our view of evil. The Psalmist is not only calling on those who love God to hate evil and injustice in the world, but he is also calling on believers to hate evil in our own lives.

Sometimes we as believers are too loving and we accept things in others that the Lord hates, because of our fear of man. Other times, we accept evil in our own lives because we simply like it. Maybe we minimize a sin like gossip, pride, jealousy or anger and only hate it when it causes us trouble rather than hating it because God hates it. What sin in your own life do you need to hate more.

Psalm 97

S—The S stands for ***Scripture***

O—The O stands for ***Observation***

A—The A stands for ***Application***

K—The K stands for ***Kneeling in Prayer***

Make a joyful noise to the Lord,
all the earth.
Psalm 98:4

Reflection Question:

Not only do we see instruments, such as trumpets and horns praising the Lord in this Psalm, but we also see nature personified as the seas and rivers and hills and trees clap their hands to the Lord. Our praise to the Lord must not be silent.

Sometimes our worship is soft and quiet but other times it should be enthusiastic. All the earth is commanded to make a joyful noise to the Lord. Are you comfortable being noisy in your worship? Why or why not? How can you be freer with your worship this week?

Psalm 98

S—The S stands for ***Scripture***

O—The O stands for ***Observation***

A—The A stands for ***Application***

K—The K stands for ***Kneeling in Prayer***

The Lord reigns;
let the peoples tremble!
He sits enthroned upon the cherubim;
let the earth quake.
Psalm 99:1

Reflection Question:

Both earth and man tremble and quake at the sight of our God reigning on his throne. God's cherubim look nothing like the religious artwork that we see of babies floating on clouds with wings. Instead, cherubim are mighty and strong angelic creatures who surround the throne of God.

Imagine for a moment the throne in heaven from Revelation 4:6-8: *"Before the throne there was as it were a sea of glass, like crystal. And around the throne, on each side of the throne, are four living creatures, full of eyes in front and behind: 7 the first living creature like a lion, the second living creature like an ox, the third living creature with the face of a man, and the fourth living creature like an eagle in flight. 8 And the four living creatures, each of them with six wings, are full of eyes all around and within, and day and night they never cease to say,"Holy, holy, holy, is the Lord God Almighty, who was and is and is to come!"*

How does reading this passage of scripture, change your reverence towards the Lord?

Psalm 99

S—The S stands for ***Scripture***

O—The O stands for ***Observation***

A—The A stands for ***Application***

K—The K stands for ***Kneeling in Prayer***

Enter his gates with thanksgiving,
and his courts with praise!
Give thanks to him;
bless his name.
Psalm 100:4

Reflection Question:

As God's people came to the temple, they were to come with hearts of thanksgiving and praise.

Our God is good, gracious, forgiving and full of mercy. He will be faithful to us forever. Because of his faithfulness and our salvation, we can give thanks to Him and praise His name forever! When you go to church, what is typically on your mind and heart? Is it thanksgiving and praise? List 5 things you are grateful for below and focus on these this Sunday, as you go to church to worship. Keep walking with the King!

Psalm 100

S—The S stands for ***Scripture***

O—The O stands for ***Observation***

A—The A stands for ***Application***

K—The K stands for ***Kneeling in Prayer***

41670828R00061

Made in the USA
Lexington, KY
10 June 2019